W9-APT-336

AmericanGirl Library®

Here's How

Published by Pleasant Company Publications
© Copyright 1996 by Pleasant Company

All rights reserved. No part of this book may be used or
reproduced in any manner whatsoever without written
permission except in the case of brief quotations embodied in
critical articles and reviews. For information, address: American
Girl Library Editor, Pleasant Company Publications, 8400 Fairway
Place, P.O. Box 620998, Middleton, Wisconsin 53562.

Printed in the United States of America.
99 00 01 02 03 04 KRH 10 9 8 7 6 5 4 3

American Girl Library® is a trademark of Pleasant Company.

Editorial Development by Jodi Evert and Jennifer Hirsch
Art Direction: Kym Abrams
Design: Tracy Hollander and Kristen Perantoni
Illustrations: Laura Cornell
Tabletop Photography: Mike Walker
Model Photography: Paul Tryba

All the instructions in this book have been tested by children
and adults. Results from their testing were incorporated into
this book. Nonetheless, all recommendations and suggestions
are made without any guarantees on the part of Pleasant
Company Publications. Because of differing tools, materials,
conditions, and individual skills, the publisher disclaims
liability for any injuries, losses, or other damages that may
result from using the information in this book.

Library of Congress Cataloging-in-Publication Data
Here's how / illustrated by Laura Cornell. — 1st ed.
p. cm. — (American girl library)
Summary: Instructions for amusements one could teach friends
or family, including reading a palm, eating with chopsticks, doing
the hula, making a coin disappear, making a French braid, learn-
ing basic sign language, and throwing a football.
ISBN 1-56247-485-5
1. Games for girls—Juvenile literature. 2. Amusements—
Juvenile literature. [1. Amusements.] I. Cornell, Laura, ill.
II. Series: American girl library (Middleton, Wis.)
GV1204.998.H47 1996 790.1'94—dc20 96-33825 CIP AC

AmericanGirl Library®

Here's How

PLEASANT
COMPANY
PUBLICATIONS™

Contents

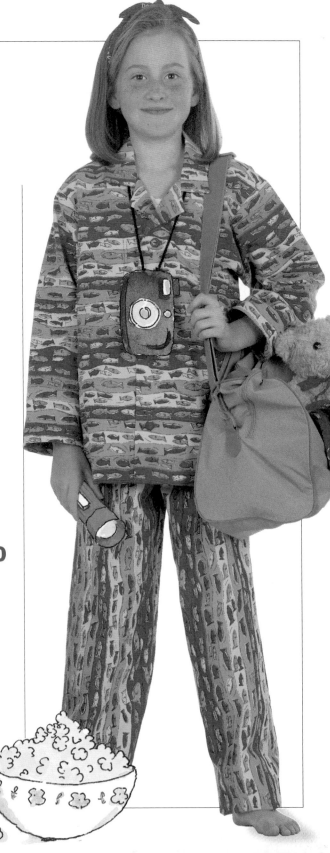

Blow Bubbles

Trouble with your bubbles? Here's help on the double!

Big, Big Bubbles

1 Chew two pieces of soft bubblegum, such as Bubblicious® or Bubble Yum®.

2 Press the gum against the back of your teeth with your tongue. Don't press the gum too flat—the thicker the gum, the bigger the bubble!

3 Push your tongue forward to make an air pocket in the gum. Blow slowly to stretch the skin of the bubble gently and evenly, so it's less likely to tear. Keep practicing, and soon you'll be blowing the biggest bubbles ever!

Double Bubbles

1 Blow a big bubble. Press your lips together to seal it.

2 Gather the rest of the gum inside your mouth and get ready to blow another bubble.

3 Push your tongue inside the bubble you've already blown. Slowly blow a small bubble. Press your lips together to seal your double bubble!

Chew your gum until there's hardly any flavor left. Then it's just right for big bubble blowing!

7

Read a Palm

Some people believe your palms show your personality.
See if you agree!

Lines

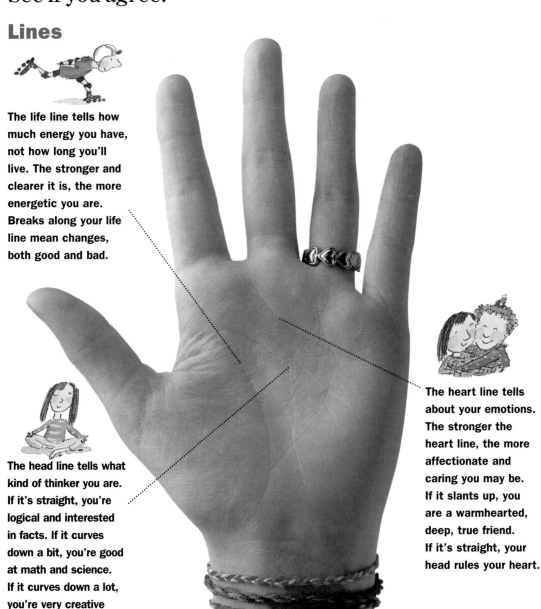

The life line tells how
much energy you have,
not how long you'll
live. The stronger and
clearer it is, the more
energetic you are.
Breaks along your life
line mean changes,
both good and bad.

The head line tells what
kind of thinker you are.
If it's straight, you're
logical and interested
in facts. If it curves
down a bit, you're good
at math and science.
If it curves down a lot,
you're very creative
and imaginative.

The heart line tells
about your emotions.
The stronger the
heart line, the more
affectionate and
caring you may be.
If it slants up, you
are a warmhearted,
deep, true friend.
If it's straight, your
head rules your heart.

Fingers

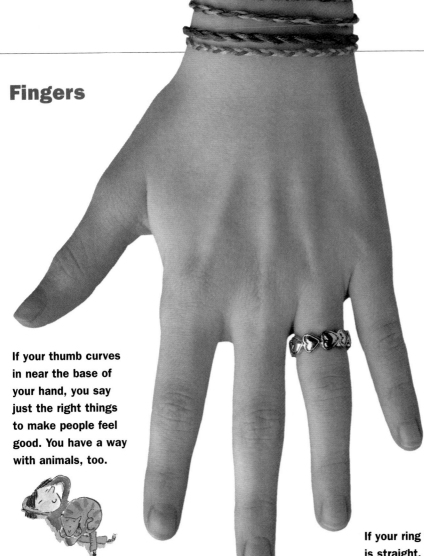

A long pinky means you're quick with words and quick to understand people. If your pinky starts lower on your palm than your other fingers, you're probably shy.

If your thumb curves in near the base of your hand, you say just the right things to make people feel good. You have a way with animals, too.

If your index finger is straight, you are a natural leader. If it is almost as long as your middle finger, you are bossy. If it's shorter than your ring finger, you'd rather follow than lead.

A straight middle finger means you're a deep thinker. If it curves, you like collecting objects better than ideas!

If your ring finger is straight, it's easy for you to show your feelings. If it's almost as long as your middle finger and longer than your index finger, you like to be the center of attention.

Eat with Chopsticks

You're in an Asian restaurant with no silverware in sight. What to do? Pick up the sticks!

1 Place the thick end of one chopstick between your thumb and index finger. Let the chopstick rest against the tip of your middle finger.

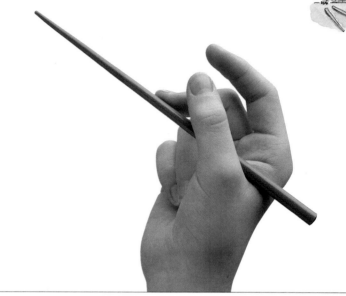

2 Hold the thick end of the second chopstick between the tips of your thumb and index finger. The bottom chopstick stays still. Move the second chopstick up and down.

3 Practice pinching small pieces of food. Then try gently pinching small clumps of rice.

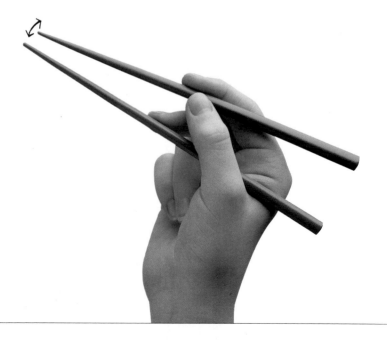

It's polite to hold your rice bowl close to your face while you eat. Leave your plate on the table.

Draw Cartoons

Create your own colorful comic strips with these loony, cartoony critters.

1 Use a soft pencil. A number 2 pencil or a "B" artist's pencil works well.

2 Hold your pencil firmly, but don't grip too hard. You'll cramp your hand.

3 Have an eraser handy. Keep it smudge-free by rubbing it on a clean piece of white paper.

A Swishy Fish

A Messy Mouse

A Peppy Puppy

A Potbelly Pig

A Pretty Kitty

A Fat Frog

Spin a Basketball

Follow three simple steps to start a winning spin!

1 Hold the basketball in the hand you write with. Bring it up in front of you about eye level and balance it on your fingertips. Your index finger should point toward you.

2 To start your spin, twist your wrist until your index finger points away from you. Let the ball spin onto your index finger. Keep your finger tilted back a bit, so the ball spins on the pad of your fingertip.

3 Use your other hand to pat the ball lightly in the direction of the spin to keep the ball turning.

Practice with a smaller basketball at first. Keep your nails clipped short for easier spinning!

15

Make a Coin Disappear!

1 Practice in private first. Place a small piece of clear two-sided tape across one corner of the handkerchief.

2 Pick up the handkerchief by the taped corner and one other corner. Show the front and back to your audience.

3 Lay the handkerchief on a table, with the taped corner near you. Place a coin in the middle of the handkerchief.

4 Fold the taped corner to the middle. Press the tape onto the coin.

5 Fold the other three corners to the middle. Ask someone to feel that the coin is still there.

6 Unfold the last corner you folded. Then pick up the taped corner, keeping the coin covered.

Wow a crowd with a coin, a handkerchief, and a sneaky little piece of two-sided tape.

7 Shake out the handkerchief and presto—no coin! Bask in the applause.

Ta dah!

Get Ready for School in 10 Minutes

The Night Before...

1 Choose what you'll wear the next day—including shoes, socks, underwear, and hair accessories and jewelry if you like.

2 Pack your backpack with homework, books, bus tickets, lunch money, and anything else you need for school. Put the backpack by the door.

3 If you'll need a coat, hat, or boots, set them by your backpack.

4 Make breakfast! Spread a bagel with peanut butter, mix fresh fruit with yogurt, and store them in the fridge. Or set aside breakfast bars, granola bars, or even leftover pizza.

5 If you want to shower, do it now!

6 Set your alarm clock. Set it five minutes earlier if you like to use the snooze button. Tomorrow, the countdown begins!

Rather snooze than cruise? Get ready the night before, and you'll soar out the door!

Get out the Door!

1 Get out of bed. Go to the bathroom and wash your hands and face. 2 minutes

2 Brush your teeth. 1 minute

3 Dress quickly. 2 minutes Brush your hair. 30 seconds

4 Eat breakfast. 4 minutes

5 Put on your coat, grab your backpack, and...

Go!

Dance the Hula

Move Your Hands

For hundreds of years, Hawaiian hula dancers have told stories with their hands. Practice these hula moves to show the people, actions, and places in your story:

Myself

Love

Island

House

Remember

Sing

Sun

Make up other moves to help tell your story. Keep them smooth, simple, and graceful. Then put the story together, letting each move flow slowly into the next.

Swish and sway, wear a lei—tell a story the Hawaiian way!

Make a Lei!

Make a *lei*, or flower necklace. Scrunch balls of colored tissue paper and string them with a needle and thread.

Move Your Feet

Now add the *vamp*, or sway:

1 Take a short step to the right, and slide your left foot over beside your right.

2 Then take a short step to the left, and slide your right foot over. Sway gently with each step. Repeat in time to music, as you tell the story with your hands.

Make a Grass Skirt!

For an easy grass skirt, tuck strips of crepe paper into the waist of a pair of shorts, and swish as you sway!

Make a French Braid

Try this terrific twist on your friends, your mom, or even your doll. Then try it on yourself!

1 Take a section of hair at the top of the head and divide it into three sections. Keep your hands close to the head, so the braid will stay tight. Put A over B, so that A is in the middle. Then put C over A, so that C is in the middle.

2 Hold the braid in one hand as shown. You can drop the middle section, as long as you hold the two sides.

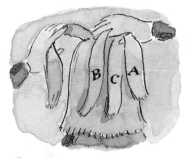

3 With your free hand, run your thumb from the side of the head up to the braid, gathering hair as you go. Add the hair to section B, keeping the braid all in one hand.

4 Take section C (the one in the middle) with your free hand and pull it to the side. Section B should now be in the middle.

5 Carefully switch hands so that the whole braid is in the other hand, and do the same thing for the other side. Keep braiding, switching hands as you switch sides.

6 When there's no more hair to add, you can end the braid or keep going with a basic braid. Put a barrette or band at the end so the braid doesn't unravel.

To be long enough to braid, hair should fall below the shoulders.

Build Forts

In a Box

1 For this outdoor fort, you'll need a big box and plenty of leaves, brush, hay, or grass clippings. Boxes that held washers, dryers, or refrigerators are perfect.

2 Turn the box upside down. Ask an adult to help you cut flaps for windows. Prop open the window flaps with sticks. Make a door flap in the same way.

3 Cover your fort from top to bottom with leaves, brush, hay, or grass clippings.

On the Beach

1 Gather a shovel, five sturdy boards, a bucket, and a big beach towel. Dig a six-foot square in the sand, about one foot deep. Pile the sand along the edges of the square to make walls. Leave an opening for the door.

2 Dig a one-foot-deep moat around the outside of the walls. Pile the sand on top of the walls.

3 Use one board for a drawbridge, and the other boards for a roof. Drape a towel over the roof boards for more shade.

Bugged by brothers? Starting a secret club? Use boxes, blankets, snow, or hay to make a private place to play!

In the Snow

1 You'll need a shovel, two wide boards, an old blanket, and a big pile of snow at least three feet deep. Dig a three-foot-wide trench in the snow. Make twists, turns, and dead ends. Pile up the snow on either side of the trench to make walls.

2 To make a door, lay the boards over the entrance to your trench. Drape the old blanket over the board, and then pile snow on top of the blanket to hold it in place.

Between Beds

1 Find a box big enough to fit over the gap between a set of twin beds. Cut out a few lookout windows. Place the box at the head of the beds. Use a blanket secured with books to cover the rest of the gap.

2 For a door, lay a broom across the foot of the beds. Drape two towels over the broomstick for curtains.

Throw like a Pro

Learn to spin a spectacular football spiral—right now!

How to Hold

1 Line up your fingers along the laces of the football. Your pinky should be near the middle of the ball.

2 Wrap your thumb around the other side of the football. Grip the ball firmly with your fingers—don't let it rest in your palm.

How to Throw

1 Try a slow throw first. Bring the football up next to your ear.

2 Lean back a bit, and shift your weight to your back leg.

3 As you start to throw, shift your weight to your front leg and straighten your arm. Just before you release the ball, snap your wrist and let the ball roll off your fingers, pinky first.

4 When you finish your throw, your arm should be out in front of you, right where you want the football to go.

Teach Your Dog to Shake, Rattle & Roll!

Three fantastic feats for Fido—show your pup how to strut her stuff!

Shake

1 Have your dog sit in front of you. Show her a treat, and then gently take one of her paws in your hand as you say "shake."

2 Give her the treat while her paw is still in your hand. Practice every day, and give her lots of praise!

Shake!

Rattle

Rattle!

1 Take your dog outside. Get her attention with a treat, and then spray her with water. Say "rattle" as she shakes off the water.

2 When she's finished, give her the treat and lots of praise. Keep practicing with her every day, until she "rattles" without water!

Roll

Roll!

1 Have your dog lie down. Say "roll" as you slowly bring a treat over her shoulders in the direction you'd like her to roll.

2 When she is on her back, help her roll with a gentle push. After she finishes her roll, reward her with the treat.

3 Keep practicing! When she has the hang of it, reward her with hugs instead of a treat!

Pack for a Super Sleepover

Invited to an overnight? Try these tips for perfect party packing!

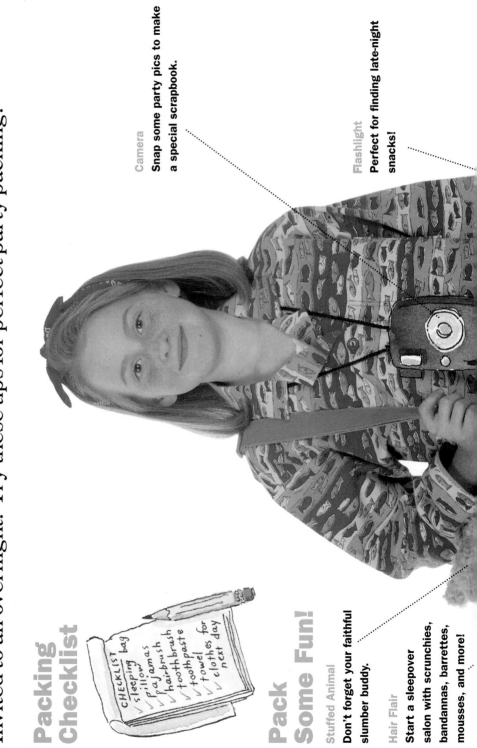

Camera
Snap some party pics to make a special scrapbook.

Flashlight
Perfect for finding late-night snacks!

Packing Checklist

CHECKLIST
✓ sleeping bag
✓ pillows
✓ pajamas
✓ hairbrush
✓ toothbrush
✓ toothpaste
✓ towel
✓ clothes for next day

Pack Some Fun!

Stuffed Animal
Don't forget your faithful slumber buddy.

Hair Flair
Start a sleepover salon with scrunchies, bandannas, barrettes, mousses, and more!

Space Saver
Save space by rolling up your pajamas, clothes for the next day, towel, and pillow in your sleeping bag. Tie it up and you're ready to travel.

Microwave Popcorn
A fun-to-eat packable treat!

Videos
Give a private showing of your favorite flicks.

Board Games
Get a board game going for after-movie madness.

Books, Tapes, and CDs
Share your favorite sounds and stories!

Spin on Skates

Skate onto the rink and learn a speedy spin in six simple steps.

1 For starters, find out which way you turn more easily by turning yourself slowly to the left and then to the right with your feet.

2 If you're spinning to the left, anchor your left toe pick. If you're spinning to the right, anchor your right toe pick.

3 Bend your knees and get in "windup" position. If you're spinning to the left, turn your shoulders a bit to the right, with your arms extended. If you're spinning to the right, turn your shoulders to the left.

4 Start with a slow spin. Straighten your knees and push off gently. At the same time, turn your shoulders in the direction of your spin. Keep your arms extended in front of you.

5 As you spin, keep your toes turned in slightly. Shift your weight to the inside edges of your skates. Your body should feel balanced and centered.

6 For a speedier spin, bring your arms in closer to your body as you turn. Try this carefully— balance is more important than speed!

To keep from getting dizzy, hold your head straight and keep your eyes looking out, not down. Try not to focus on anything in particular.

33

Juggle Scarves

One

1 Hold one scarf in your *dominant hand*—the hand you write with.

2 To toss the scarf, scoop your scarf hand from outside to inside. Let go of the scarf when your hand is at chest height. Catch the scarf in your other hand and stop.

3 Now toss the scarf back to your dominant hand. Practice tossing it back and forth. Notice the figure-eight pattern the scarf makes as you toss it.

Two

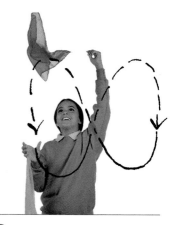

1 Hold one scarf in each hand, palm down.

2 Toss one scarf in the air, just as you did before. When that scarf begins to come down, toss the other scarf. Catch both scarves and stop.

3 Toss the scarves back and forth until you can do it smoothly. Again, notice the figure-eight pattern. Practice until you are comfortable starting with either hand.

Three breezy scarves help you juggle with ease!

Three!

1 Hold two scarves in your dominant hand and one scarf in your other hand.

2 Toss one of the scarves in your dominant hand into the air. When that scarf begins to come down, toss the scarf from your other hand into the air.

3 As you catch the first scarf, toss the third scarf in the air. Always keep one scarf in the air. Keep tossing and catching until you have a steady rhythm.

Use chiffon scarves—they float the best!

Tell Fortunes

Use this crazy contraption to share funny fortunes with your friends!

To Make It

1 You'll need a piece of white paper at least eight inches square. Fold in the four corners.

2 Turn over the paper. Fold in the four corners on this side.

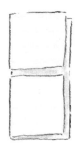

3 Fold this side in half from left to right. Make a sharp crease, and then unfold the paper.

4 Fold this side in half again, this time from top to bottom. Make a sharp crease, and then unfold the paper.

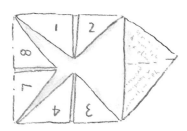

5 Write a number from 1 to 8 on each of the eight triangles. Then write a silly fortune on the back of each triangle.

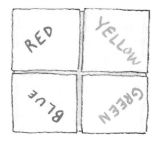

6 Turn over the paper and write a color on each of the four squares.

To Work It

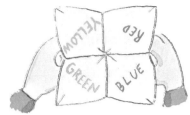

1 Hold the fortune-teller in your hand, numbers up. Fold it from bottom to top. The numbers will now be inside the fortune-teller.

2 Slip your thumbs and index fingers underneath the color squares, so you're holding your fortune-teller like this.

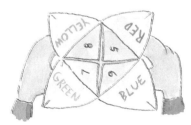

3 To open, pinch the fortune-teller between your fingers and thumbs. Move your hands apart sideways until you see four numbers inside. Then close the fortune-teller.

4 Now press your index fingers together and your thumbs together. Move your index fingers up and your thumbs down. You'll see the other four numbers inside. Close it again. Repeat Steps 3 and 4 until you can do them smoothly.

To Tell a Fortune

1 Ask a friend to pick one of the four colors. Spell out the color, making one motion for each letter.

2 Then ask your friend to pick one of the numbers inside. Move the fortune-teller that many times.

3 Now ask your friend to pick another one of the numbers inside. Lift up the triangle with that number and read your friend her fortune!

Jump Double Dutch

Turning the Ropes

1 Stand straight, with your elbows close to your sides. Hold the ropes with your thumbs on top. Back away from your turning partner until the ropes are stretched straight.

2 Start turning the ropes in small, inward circles, like an eggbeater. Slowly move toward your partner until the ropes slap the ground as they turn.

Getting In

1 Stand close to one of the turners' shoulders. Listen to the rhythm of the ropes.

2 When the back rope slaps the ground, run into the middle of the ropes. Get ready to jump—the front rope comes around quickly!

Rope a few friends into a fast-paced game of Double Dutch. Twice the ropes means twice the fun!

Staying In

1 Always jump on the balls of your feet. Keep your knees close together and your arms at your sides so they don't get tangled in the ropes.

Getting Out

1 Face one of the rope turners. As you exit, you'll move past the turner's shoulder.

2 Take one jump toward the turner, and then quickly step out of the ropes.

Build a Castle of Cards

Be the queen of your very own castle! All you need are steady hands and a deck of old playing cards.

1 Begin with two cards. Lean two short edges together to form a little tent.

2 Take four more cards and make walls around the sides of the tent.

3 Add two cards on top to make a roof.

4 Take two more cards and form a tent. Slide the second tent into the space between the roof cards of the first tent.

5 Build walls around the second tent. Add two cards on top to make a roof.

6 When you have a few tents built together, start a second story. If your castle crumbles, rebuild it! The more you practice, the better you'll get.

Build your castle on a carpet. The cards will stand up more easily than if you build on a smooth tabletop.

41

Study Handwriting

People called *graphologists* believe penmanship tells a lot about personality. Find out if you agree with the experts!

slant

Do your letters slant to the *left*? You're probably a little shy. If they slant to the *right*, you're outgoing and friendly. Straight *up* and *down* letters mean you're straightforward with people—you say what you mean and mean what you say!

t's

Look at the bars on your lowercase *t*'s. Bars that slant up mean you have high goals for yourself. If they're straight across, you're confident. Bars that slant down mean you're a rebel and a fighter—and you're not afraid to show it!

Loops

Are your *loops* tall and round? You probably love being the center of attention. If you write tall and skinny loops, you don't have to buy a lot of things to be happy. Short, round *loops* mean you have good concentration and are cautious. Really narrow *loops* mean you can't stand clutter.

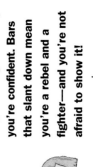

i's

Where do you dot your lowercase *i*? To the right? You're a quick thinker. To the left? You have a tendency to put things off. Right above the *i*? You crave perfection!

Dear Aunt Lisa,

Thank you for my photo album. I've filled half of it with pictures from my birthday party. There's a great picture of you and

Press

How hard do you press when you write? If your letters are light, you're gentle and relaxed. Pressing hard means you're energetic and forceful. No one better get in your way! A medium press means you're right in the middle—not too laid-back or too pushy.

Do a Dive

Practice a plop, and then try a drop. Work up to a stand for a dive that's simply grand!

Plop

1 Sit at the side of the deep end of a pool, with your legs dangling into the water. Hold your arms out in front of you and aim the top of your head at the water.

2 Lean forward and plop into the water headfirst. Practice this over and over until you feel very comfortable doing it.

Drop

1 Crouch at the side of the deep end with your legs about shoulder-width apart. Line up your big toes along the edge of the pool. Hold your arms out in front of you and look down at the bottom of the pool.

2 Lean forward and drop into the pool headfirst, just as you did before. Practice, practice, practice!

Stand

1 Stand at the side of the deep end, with one foot slightly behind the other. Line up the big toe of your front foot with the edge of the pool. Hold your arms out in front of you and look down at the bottom of the pool.

2 Slowly let yourself fall into the pool headfirst. As you practice, try gently pushing off from the side of the pool as you dive. You'll start to dive out a bit, instead of straight down.

Always, always, always practice diving in the *deep* end of a pool. Never practice in the shallow end or in a lake.

Learn the Language of Signing

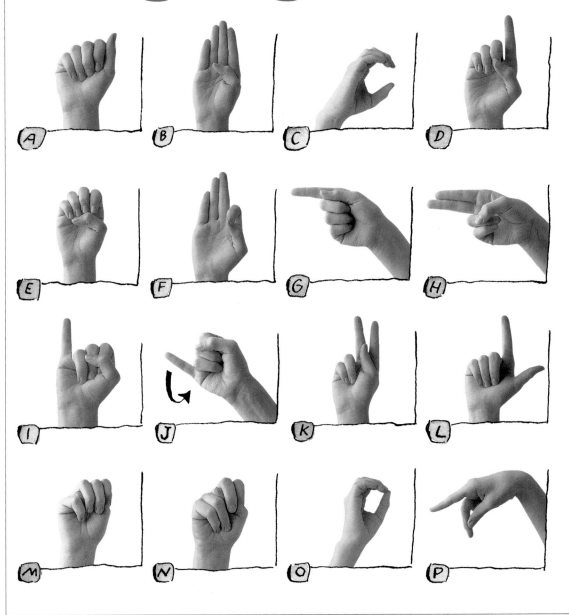

Some call sign language "the language of the hands."
Some say it's like making words dance!

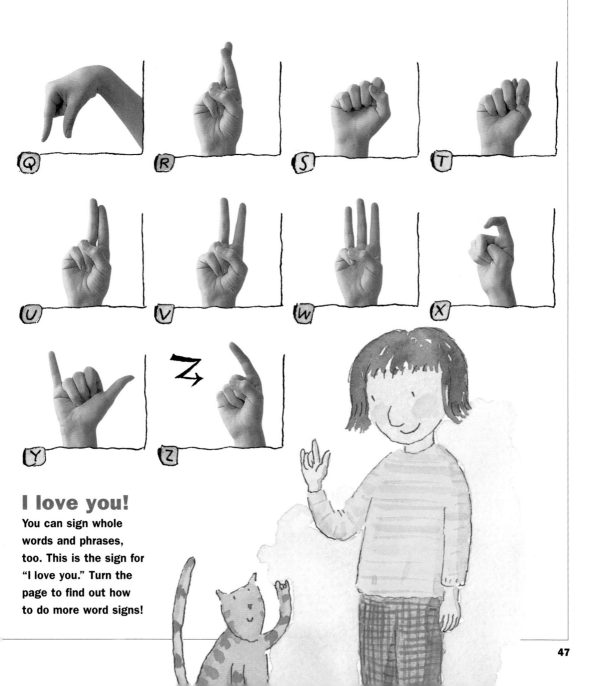

I love you!
You can sign whole
words and phrases,
too. This is the sign for
"I love you." Turn the
page to find out how
to do more word signs!

Share these graceful, silent signals with your family and friends.

Fun

Both hands form the letter H. Touch right hand to nose and then place it back on the left hand.

Play

Both hands form the letter Y. Wiggle them up and down a few times.

Hug

Both hands form the letter S. Cross arms across chest as if you're hugging something.

Friend

Link index fingers, first with the right index finger on top, and then the left.

Family

Both hands form the letter F, palms facing each other. Move your hands so your palms face you, with your pinkies touching.

Girl

Right hand forms the letter A. Place thumb on right cheek and move down twice.

The

Form a T with your right hand. Twist out.

End!

Move top hand along bottom hand until it drops off the edge.